How To Set Healthy Boundaries For Children

7 Simple Steps For Teaching Children Boundaries

Frank Dixon

from various sources. Please consult a licensed professional before attempting any techniques outlined in this book.

By reading this document, the reader agrees that under no circumstances is the author responsible for any losses, direct or indirect, that are incurred as a result of the use of the information contained within this document, including, but not limited to, errors, omissions, or inaccuracies.

Before we begin, I have something special waiting for you. An action-packed 1 page printout with a few quick & easy tips taken from this book that you can start using today to become a better parent right now!

It's my gift to you, free of cost. Think of it as my way of saying thank you to you for purchasing this book.

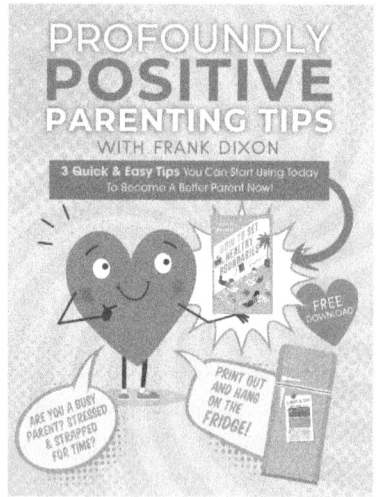

Claim your download of Profoundly Positive Parenting with Frank Dixon by scanning the QR code below and join my mailing list.

Sign up below to grab your free copy, print it out and hang it on the fridge!

Sign Up By Scanning The QR Code With Your Phone's Camera To Be Redirected To A Page To Enter Your Email And Receive INSTANT Access To Your Download

Before we jump in, I'd like to express my gratitude. I know this mustn't be the first book you came across and yet you still decided to give it a read. There are numerous courses and guides you could have picked instead that promise to make you an ideal and well-rounded parent while raising your children to be the best they can be.

But for some reason, mine stood out from the rest and this makes me the happiest person on the planet right now. If you stick with it, I promise this will be a worthwhile read.

In the pages that follow, you're going to learn the best parenting skills so that your child can grow to become the best version of themselves and in doing so experience a meaningful understanding of what it means to be an effective parent.

Notable Quotes About Parenting

"Children Must Be Taught How To Think, Not What To Think."

— Margaret Mead

"It's easier to build strong children than to fix broken men [or women]."

- Frederick Douglass

"Truly great friends are hard to find, difficult to leave, and impossible to forget."

— George Randolf

"Nothing in life is to be feared, it is only to be understood. Now is the time to understand more, so that we may fear less."

— Scientist Marie Curie

Table of Contents

Introduction

How many times have you wanted to say no in answer to your child's unreasonable demand, only to give in and say yes instead?

Probably more times than you'd care to admit.

As parents, especially of today's generation, we often fall victim to the fear that if we say no to our children, they will start hating us. We fear they will learn to live without us and not come back to visit once they leave the nest. We don't want the label of a *bad parent* stuck on our backs, with other parents judging our skills when our child throws a temper tantrum at the grocery store. In the quest for perfect parenthood, however, we sometimes forget the kind of role model we should aspire to be for our children.

Every time we say yes to them for something unreasonable, it sets the wrong example. Children see that they can get away with anything they want in life if they make a little fuss, act out, and cause a scene. The danger here is that this behavior can carry on as they grow, resulting in them becoming the kind of selfish individual who believes that they are entitled to have anything their heart desires, regardless of others' feelings. As they enter adulthood and are hit by the realities of work, life, and romantic relationships, they become dumbfounded when anyone denies their request.

Learning to set healthy boundaries early therefore is pivotal for a child's empathic development. You want to raise someone that you are proud of, that acknowledges and respects others' needs for personal space, and that knows when they should say no without fear of rejection, shame, or guilt.

So what exactly *is* a boundary?

In the simplest of terms, a boundary is where one thing ends and another begins. A personal boundary is a limit that an individual sets to define what they allow and don't allow, what they will and won't do, what behaviors they will tolerate and what they won't.

All humans, whether they know it or not, have boundaries at the extreme limits of what they can stand. When the body reaches its physical limit, it experiences pain. When an emotional boundary is breached, we experience emotional pain, anger, and stress. Some people are experts at pushing themselves to their limits, but no one can get rid of their most extreme boundaries entirely, and the very act of even *reaching* these inherent boundaries can result in lasting trauma. Most people have self-imposed boundaries within the limits of the more extreme inherent ones to avoid this (such as lifting weights until your arms feel tired rather than lifting weights until your arms are physically damaged).

Like adults, children have boundaries too; they just likely aren't aware of them. They might lack experience with the world, with interpersonal relationships, or with the way they themselves react physically or emotionally to stress. Despite being told that it is wrong to bite or hit others, children do. Despite being told that they mustn't talk to strangers, they're inclined to start up a conversation with anyone they find interesting out of sheer curiosity.

Setting healthy boundaries for children is therefore extremely important. They must learn the behaviors that are allowed, acceptable, and tolerable, and the behaviors that are not. Healthy boundaries assist children in building essential life skills like patience, resourcefulness, problem-solving, discipline, and responsibility. It makes them more resilient and independent. When they learn to say no, they learn self-care. They learn to put their needs first and to prioritize themselves. Since parents are a child's first teacher in the school of how the world works, the responsibility rests on them to teach children how to set healthy boundaries. Parents can help children understand the many written and unwritten rules that make up society right from home; the home is a child's first exposure to the world, and can serve as a kind of miniature trial version of the wider world and how it works. Setting healthy boundaries can help children integrate themselves more easily and healthily into social situations that they encounter as they grow up.

A lack of boundaries has the potential to cause one of two extreme problems later in life. On the one hand, children that lack an understanding of the boundaries of others may become entitled and privileged as they grow. They might become surprised or upset when they're told 'no' or are denied what they want, and they might not treat other people with the respect they deserve.

The other issue that might arise from a child not understanding boundaries is a potential lack of awareness of their own needs and limits. For example, children who don't know how to set boundaries and who don't know what is and isn't appropriate touch are at higher risk for being abused without even understanding what abuse is. Even in a less extreme example, a child who doesn't know how to say 'no' might find themselves in a situation where they're overwhelmed by all the responsibilities they've reluctantly agreed to. Both situations can have lasting negative impacts on a child as they grow.

Therefore it is essential that children learn to establish healthy boundaries early on. It helps them and others around them to feel safe and comfortable in their own skin.

The goal of this guide is to equip parents with the right tools and strategies to start the conversation of setting healthy boundaries with their children. The following seven steps will help to define the word boundary, discuss its many facets, instill the importance of the concept, and foster discussions that are important for the development of both parents and kids.

Chapter 1:

Knowing When to Say No

Healthy boundaries allow children the freedom to be who they want to be, and can help them cater to their own needs as well as the needs of others. Raising children to be empathetic towards each other promotes healthy relationships; they learn when to say no without feeling pressured, to refuse things with dignity, and to accept rejection gracefully.

Even adults can find setting healthy boundaries to be a difficult thing at times. We fear that if we resist, hold back, or refuse someone's needs, we won't be loved or valued. As a result we might overbook our schedules, stay late to finish someone else's work, or offer a helping hand despite being tired to the bone. What we fail to realize is that our children are watching us. Such an act may seem a simple gesture of kindness, but it also sets an example of a role model putting others before their own basic needs. And while acts of kindness should be encouraged, it's also important to demonstrate that such acts should not come at the cost of one's own physical or mental health.

Everyone has experienced something like this. Imagine a spouse informing you at the last minute that they're having important colleagues over for dinner when the house is in a state. Imagine the stress of having to say no to a boss who wants you to stay late when you have responsibilities at home to attend to. Or imagine yourself back in high school, undergoing peer pressure to try alcohol or another substance you know you shouldn't. These are all examples of scenarios where a strong sense of one's own boundaries is incredibly helpful, and situations both you and your child will likely undergo at some point.

Lacking boundaries is unhealthy; it is a drain on your physical and mental well-being. It takes away power from you and gives it to someone else. When you don't set healthy boundaries, you allow others to take advantage of you and put yourself at risk of an abuse of power. Your children see that and learn to take on the same stress, assuming that it is healthy and normal. They say yes to every expectation without knowing if they will be able to fulfill it or not. They overbook and overcommit, and then worry and feel anxious when they've stretched themselves too thin. It's why the ability to say no is so very important, and a lesson that needs to be taught at a young age.

Understanding Healthy Boundaries

The benefits to setting healthy boundaries for children don't stop there. Boundaries help to improve discipline, as rules are clearly laid out and discussed in advance. Kids with a good sense of what is and isn't appropriate are much less likely to get into trouble. In addition, research has shown that children feel insecure when they don't know the limits or rules of a situation; unpredictability confuses them (Sandstrom & Huerta, 2013). Not knowing what is expected of them or what behaviors will result in rewards and consequences makes learning and habit formation harder. For example, if they don't know *why* they should hold your hand when crossing the road, they might not understand the risk of crossing the road and put themselves in danger. Therefore as a parent you must set healthy boundaries so that children are clear on the expectations you and others have for them and can develop an understanding for how to live up to those expectations. In short, boundaries give kids a sense of security and confidence.

Another reason children need limits and boundaries is so that they can avoid becoming anxious when others don't act the way they expect them to. For example, imagine your child makes an unfair request. Let's say they're poking you repeatedly, desperate for you to buy them an ice cream from the ice cream truck when they haven't eaten any of their vegetables. If you were in a good mood or perhaps distracted by something else, you might say yes and give them money for the ice cream. The child has now made the connection that their demands will be met if they pester you enough. Then, a few weeks later, they pull the same trick with the aunt that's babysitting; the aunt says no, since the child is being rude for poking and pestering her. This can result in confusion and anxiety, since the same behavior was rewarded in one instance and punished in another.

Having boundaries prevents conflicts; when rules and routines are present and clearly defined, there is little room for argument or backtalk to happen. The child knows what they are and aren't allowed to do, and hopefully tries to stay within those limits. Testing boundaries is a part of every child's development, but having the rules and consequences lined up ahead of time cuts down on argument and conflict in addition to helping children understand the repercussions of ignoring or testing established rules. Healthy boundaries help to steer behaviors towards those that will help them to succeed later in life.

Perhaps most importantly, boundaries also keep children safe. Understanding *why* they shouldn't talk to strangers or cross the road without looking will help them to make good decisions when you're not around to guide them, resulting in a safer child and a more relaxed parent.

When children respect the boundaries that their parents, teachers, and other adults set for them, they grow into compassionate and empathetic individuals who respect the needs of others as well as their own. They are less likely to pry into the matters of others because they know the importance of personal space, and they are more likely to be nice and respectful to the people around them. Not knowing how to respond when someone appears to be anxious, in distress, or irritated ends up making adult life a lot harder.

Boundaries help children cope with the many negative and uncomfortable emotions they will experience while growing up. The primary reason why some parents avoid setting boundaries for their children is that they think denying their kids things will make them mad or sad. These parents forget that as children grow they will have to face many situations where they will feel mad or sad. So wouldn't it be a better use of time to use boundaries to teach them how to deal with those emotions when they arise on their own?

Building emotional intelligence is an important and much needed skill today. It's vital to teach children how to cope with difficult emotions without giving in to their every request. If they want a cookie and can't get it because the shops are closed, let them experience, label, and acknowledge the frustration and anger they feel inside them. Once they are done crying, whining, or screaming about it, sit down with them and calmly talk about the episode they just had, why their reaction was inappropriate for the situation, and what would make them feel better (other than the cookie).

Do I Need to Set Healthy Boundaries for My Children?

Many parents are unaware of the need for boundaries for their children. They let kids be kids and don't see a lack of boundaries as a hindrance to their independence and growth. If you don't think your child needs to learn about boundaries and limits, here are a few scenarios which may change your mind. You might even end up relating to a few of them and realize how easy it is for children to abuse someone's personal space without even understanding what they're doing.

Scenario 1

You are chatting with a friend at their house with your children when suddenly you hear your younger one yell "Mom, they have Jell-O!" You acknowledge the remark and get back to chatting. A minute later you hear a crash. You turn around to find your two children eating Jell-O straight from the refrigerator while its door is open, and there's a carton of eggs broken on the ground. Your children's faces are covered with jelly, and they don't seem to think they have done anything wrong despite the fact that they've taken food from your friend without asking *and* caused a mess for your friend to clean up.

Scenario 2

You receive a call from your son's teacher saying that your son mistreated another child in class. You find out that he tried to forcefully feed a friend of his the sandwich you made him for lunch. The child being fed was uncomfortable, started crying, and reported it to the teacher. When you confront your son he replies "but she said she was hungry!" Although your child's intentions were pure, the way he invaded his friend's personal space and paid no regard for her lack of consent wasn't right.

Scenario 3

You just told your child that you will be in the bathroom for a minute, and that they should stay put in the lounge. A minute later they open the door unannounced and start to have a conversation with you while you are on the toilet. You try to explain that you wanted to do your business in peace, but your child doesn't understand or respect your need to be alone just for a minute.

Scenario 4

You are at the grocery store with your child, and they are creating a scene by touching everything in the aisles. They are all over the place, tearing the packaging off things and eating fruit right out from the basket. The scene attracts an employee, who is forced to charge you for items you weren't intending to buy due to their being ruined.

Scenario 5

The yelling and screaming continues as your child refuses to get in bed unless they are in their favorite jammies. But the jammies are in the laundry, since your child got ice cream all over them yesterday. You have to explain that no matter how much fuss your child makes, the jammies won't be done drying until tomorrow. The screaming has woken up the baby brother, who was just successfully put to sleep and will now be up for another hour.

All these scenarios suggest a lack of respect for boundaries on the child's part.

A lack of healthy boundaries can lead to conflict and back-talking, as a child might feel as if they have a right to bother others for any reason they like. Conversely, it can also lead to a lack of understanding of what's appropriate for others to do to them. This can result in the child becoming hurt, sexually harassed, or psychologically violated. Both outcomes can be avoided through early intervention and ongoing discussion of limits and boundaries at a level appropriate to the child's age. Read on to learn about seven steps parents can take to achieve just that.

Chapter 2:

Explaining Personal Space

to a Child

Ever had someone stand so close to you that you can smell their breakfast or count the number of teeth they have? Gross and uncomfortable, indeed!

As grownups, we know that extreme closeness to a stranger isn't something most people are comfortable with. Major invasions of personal space can even be reported as harassment, especially in the workplace. But how would we define personal space to someone who has never heard of the concept? Is it something like an invisible hula hoop that one carries around their waist? Is it something that goes away if you're familiar with the other person? When do we need to be aware of others' personal space while in public?

Little kids are naturally curious, and one of their favorite games might be touching everything within reach. From grabbing a handful of mom's hair to flipping a light switch on and off just because it's there, kids are drawn towards new textures and objects that they can interact with and learn about through touch.

This curiosity extends to interpersonal touch, which might include anything from unannounced hugging to kissing, poking, slapping, and licking things and people. There is a time and place to be curious and to explore the world of touch, but youngsters don't come pre-programmed with a list of what's appropriate to touch and what's off limits.

How did our parents prevent us from touching things and people we shouldn't have? How did they teach us about boundaries? A harsh no, perhaps, or yanking the offending hand away, or even a firm slap on the wrist? Perhaps consequences more severe than that? Though the scolding may have been severe, for most of us it seemed to work; we realized that the sooner we learned to maintain and respect each other's personal space, the more likely we were to be respected in turn.

The question is this: How do we go about teaching our children the same lessons without resorting to the corporal punishment that may have been used on us as kids?

The first step to setting healthy boundaries is ensuring that children understand exactly *what* they are. A clear and understandable definition will help to clear up confusion and avoid misinterpretation. Simply put, personal space is something that everyone has a right to. It's a space where one feels unthreatened and safe, and a space that each individual has complete control over.

Personal space comes in two varieties, tangible and intangible. The tangible space is the physical space around us whereas the intangible space is the conceptual and psychological space around us. Maintaining tangible personal space is easier than intangible personal space. In tangible personal space, you have physical guidelines about maintaining distance as you approach, interact, and talk to someone. Picture an invisible hula hoop or hamster ball establishing the area around a person that others are not allowed to enter without permission. Conversely, it can be hard to determine everyone's need for *intangible* space as there isn't a tool to measure it. Intangible space includes understanding body language, respecting someone's need for alone time, and not invading someone's privacy by asking personal questions.

Mastering the concepts of both tangible and intangible can be tricky for youngsters, but it will help them to become compassionate, sensible, and assertive individuals.

How to Begin

Direct instruction as well as visual and verbal cues can help young children understand the importance of respecting one another's personal space. You can begin with defining to them what personal space is, and then role-play situations where respecting personal space is the goal. For example, you can stand very close to them and speak and then ask them if they felt uncomfortable or not. Then you can move a small distance away and then ask again how they feel. Change up the situation so that you are now pretending to be a stranger, a teacher, a friend, a family member, or some other adult your child might encounter. Establish that there should be different rules for different people.

Teach them social cues where they judge the reactions of others around them and form an analysis about how comfortable or uncomfortable the other person feels. For example, ask them to notice how a person feels when they speak to them. Do they seem mad, irritated, annoyed? Do they seem to back away or cross their arms to their chest to maintain some distance? Do they avoid making eye contact or look elsewhere? Do they take space back and readjust their position? Does their body go stiff? Do they squirm or fidget?

All these are telltale signs for how a person might feel around your child. Paying attention to these social cues should help them to readjust their position and give the other person the physical space they need.

In a similar vein, teach your child that they also deserve their privacy when they want it. When they are old enough to use the restroom by themselves, encourage them to close the door or keep it only slightly ajar because they deserve privacy. Similarly, if they are old enough to change their clothes themselves, volunteer to leave the room while they do so that they understand the importance of their private time. By respecting your child's privacy, you teach them in turn to respect others'.

When they say no to an interaction such as being tickled by you, immediately stop and respect their decision. If they feel hesitant in shaking someone's hand, don't force them to. If they feel uncomfortable sitting in their grandfather's lap, don't make them. If they don't want to be touched while bathing, respect that. All these little gestures will tell them that their need for privacy is a valued right.

Validate their feelings when they come up to you to tell you that they have been pushed, touched, or made uncomfortable by someone. Don't brush their feelings aside, and don't minimize their experience. This especially applies to young girls, who are still sometimes told that if a boy is mean to them or touches them, it must mean he likes her. Make sure that she knows that her body is hers, and that no one should touch her without her permission.

Always ask if your child is okay with a hug or kiss before giving them one. This will empower them to take control of the type of boundaries they want around themselves. Respect their right to say no, and don't feel hurt if they turn you down.

Activities to Encourage Respecting Personal Space

Many children learn better when they don't know they are being taught. When learning is coupled with play, it can better promote recall and memory later. In this section we will look at three different activities that encourage children to respect personal boundaries while they're experiencing new and fun activities.

Hula Hoop Bubble

We mentioned this activity earlier while discussing personal space; the activity is simple and requires one hula hoop for each person playing. The goal of the game is to teach children about maintaining a respectful distance from others. Simply place the hula hoop around your waist and ask your child to do the same. Tell them that the space between them and the hula hoop is their personal space that no one has a right to invade. Call it a hula hoop bubble, and have fun bouncing off of each other's bubble. Then, remove the hula hoop and ask them to simply imagine it's there while you continue bouncing off each other. Ask to enter their bubble, and only do so if the child says yes. Explain to them that the hula hoop bubble is the appropriate amount of distance they must maintain from others unless they have been given permission to enter someone else's bubble.

Carpet Squares

Another great exercise is to take them shopping for carpet samples in patterns they feel drawn to. Try to find a piece large enough for your child to sit on comfortably; stitch two pieces together if you need to. This carpet square is now their special space. Tell them that no one is allowed to step onto the carpet, not even you. Encourage sitting on the carpet as they do their homework, arts and crafts, reading, or watching TV. Get one for yourself and place it a respectable distance from theirs, if you like. Explain to them that the square represents their personal space that only they can occupy and that everyone will respect should they want some no-touch time.

Personal Space Corner

To further encourage the idea of personal space, designate a corner in the house where they can go when they need some time alone. This can be a reading area, a balcony, or a room under the stairs. Tell your child that they can do whatever they feel like doing when in the corner. You or anyone else is not to disturb them when they are in that zone except in an emergency. This will increase their understanding of personal space both tangible and intangible. As they grow older, tell them that their room is now their personal space and that no one should enter without knocking and asking permission. This also applies to you and your room as well as any other family members' personal spaces.

Chapter 3:

Creating Rules and

Structure

Kids need structure and routines in order to develop soundly. They need firm rules and conditions for rewards and consequences. Ask an expert about sleep training your child, or an educator about how to help your child do well in school, or a behavioral expert about how to effectively discipline your child, and they will all tell you to provide your child with a regular and predictable routine. Pretty much all the learning that a child does in the early developmental years of their lives comes from the structure and routine they have at home.

It makes sense. The world out there is scary for them; everything is new and exciting. How can you help them to be aware of the complexities and dangers of certain situations when they might be too young to understand that the dangers even exist? With structure and solid rules in place, children feel safe and reassured. They can trust others around them, accept things as they are, make sense of their surroundings, and learn to make friends.

With rules come limits and boundaries. When a rule is disobeyed, there is a consequence that follows. The consequence represents the abuse of a boundary or limit that was created for them. Structure in a child's life helps them set expectations, and helps parents convey that expectation clearly. It allows parents to encourage good behavior as well as talk about and administer constraints and consequences.

There are many other reasons to have rules for children, but perhaps the most important is to help children develop the ability to manage their behaviors, which is a skill no child is too young to learn. As they grow, their interactions will increase in number and complexity, and they will be introduced to all sorts of people and experience different social gatherings where they must behave in a disciplined and respectful way. Without rules and proper structure this seems almost impossible. Children can acquire self-control if their parents impose certain rules on them. Over time, these rules turn into lifelong habits that stay with them forever; starting early with setting healthy boundaries is therefore the best way to go about it.

According to Lisa Damour, a psychologist who specializes in counseling teenage girls, many studies have revealed that although children need both affection and discipline to grow up into well-adjusted adults, the latter is more important. Discipline and rules give them the tools they will eventually rely on to succeed in the real world. This doesn't mean that children don't deserve affection; it simply means that if you want them to be happy, you have to teach them some discipline too so that they can act responsibly.

Essentials of Rule Setting

As stated earlier, children can't manage themselves at first. They need some assistance from their parents to live up to societal norms. As you begin to set limits and create rules in the house, there are a few things to be aware of.

Rules, no matter how simple or complex, should be clear. They should be easy to follow. Clear rules set clear expectations and prevent confusion and misinterpretation. If a rule is unclear or hard to understand, try to simplify it.

Secondly, rules should be consistent. The consequences should remain the same every time a rule is broken, and there shouldn't be any exceptions or leniency shown by either of the parents. Consistent rules turn into habits; when children are aware of the consequences, they don't try to take unfair advantage of situations. Following similar rules as the role model helps to encourage good behavior at all times.

When discussing rules, make sure not to overwhelm your children with more than what they can handle. Begin with two or three basic rules in the beginning and take note of how they fare with those. For instance, if they are young, you may want to start with basic rules like 'no throwing food' or 'no hitting'.

When setting rules, set realistic expectations for your child. Don't expect your child to follow a rule that encourages a behavior they can't control. You can't expect them to not cry when they're upset or emotional; it may not be something they can prevent. Similarly, don't expect them to simply stop being anxious or scared in a new or frightening situation. Rules should only limit behaviors, never feelings.

Have the consequences for breaking a rule clearly defined, and be consistent with them. Your child should always be aware of what will happen if a rule is broken. The consequence should match the severity of the broken rule. Some examples of consequences might include extra chores, no dessert, a cancelled playdate, or a temporarily suspended privilege such as TV time.

Describe examples of misbehavior when you're outlining rules. Instead of a nebulous rule such as 'don't misbehave', have specific rules like 'don't push your sister' or 'don't throw food'. The clearer you are in terms of your expectations, the easier they will be for your child to follow.

This also applies to explaining the expected behavior and offering alternatives to bad habits. 'Don't push your sister' goes hand-in-hand with 'ask politely for someone to move out of your way'. Again, the goal is to make things obvious for children so that they know what is and isn't expected of them.

Next, learn to pick your battles. Do you want to start a temper tantrum over some toys that your children forgot to put back in their place? Overlook unimportant misbehavior and focus on more important ones. You want them to hear what you say, but if you are saying too much at once, they might forget or miss some of it. Therefore, try to focus more on building new skills than on eliminating older ones. Once they learn new skills they will naturally forget the older habits.

Give the highest priority to rules about safety and protection. You want to ensure that they understand why they shouldn't cross the road by themselves, why they shouldn't run away, and why they shouldn't talk to strangers. Make sure they know that their safety is the most important thing in any given situation.

Activities and Exercises to Create Structure

Teaching children how to follow rules and how to abide by routines is pivotal. Below are some ideas that you can use as inspiration to help young ones comprehend the need for rules and structure in their lives.

Get Them Involved

When creating house rules, don't exclude your children from the process. Instead, ask them to join in and listen to their suggestions. Set expectations after discussing them with your children so that they don't feel that the rules are unfair or unjust. You can also ask them to brainstorm any new ideas to be turned into house rules and see what they come up with. Once you have a list of rules, have them painted or drawn on a poster and place the poster where it is easily visible. For example, if there is a rule that they can't get into bed unless they have brushed their teeth and gotten into their jammies, have that rule on a poster or sheet of paper installed in their room or by the door. You can also add a column of consequences where you list what they will have to give up or do if they don't follow said rule.

Have Them Help Enforce Rules

To instill the importance of rule-setting and routine, let children take control of the rule-making process and police anyone that tries to break a rule. For example, if no one is allowed to bring their phone to bed and your child notices your spouse doing so, your child can call them out and enact an appropriate consequence. If there is more than one child in the house, allow each of them the chance to be the rule police so that they can all learn to abide by the rules.

Set Rewards

Rewards have the potential to be even more encouraging of rule-following than consequences. Add a column to your rule chart that lists rewards that can be earned by, for example, following a rule for a whole week without any reminders. Make sure to follow through on these rewards, and to reinforce the idea that they're receiving this reward for following a specific rule or behavior.

Chapter 4:

Show and Teach Respect

A strong sense of personal boundaries informs the way we handle the responsibilities that we have towards ourselves and others. We must ensure that people feel comfortable around us and that they don't feel invalidated or left out. We must respect their differences and embrace diversity. Setting healthy boundaries allows us to interact with all people in a safe and secure environment where they feel valued, listened to, and accepted.

How we treat others is often determined by the way we want to be treated. Our treatment of others is also influenced by our inherent thoughts and positive and negative biases towards them. Everyone has biases they aren't aware of, and while we may not be able to control those biases, we can work to overcome them in our interactions.

Boundaries may seem like limits, but in actual fact they are the one thing that sets us free. They allow us to be ourselves and allow others to be themselves. They promote respect and free speech, the sharing of ideas, stories about different cultures, and understanding each other's strengths and weaknesses. Healthy boundaries form a permeable barrier between us and others; well-placed boundaries allow you to be more assertive, authentic, outspoken, and courageous. Through them you can take ownership of your actions and feelings.

A child is new to the world, and will naturally be inquisitive as to how the world works. I'm sure every parent has dealt with the incessant question of 'why' being thrown at them every other minute! A child's questioning and curiosity multiplies when they come across someone or something that seems different from themselves and what they're used to. If someone has a different opinion or a different way of doing things, a child will probably want to know why. This is where you can begin to teach kids about diversity and its importance, and discuss how to accept differences in others with patience and openness. You must teach them that it is our uniqueness that makes us special, and that regardless of where someone comes from, what they look like, or what they do, we all deserve kindness and respect equally.

Patience and Respecting Differences

We all want our kids to grow up in a world free from discrimination and bias. We want them to see and treat every human being with respect regardless of where they come from or how they look. As stated earlier, this is only possible when we teach them how to respect others' boundaries and accept others' opinions and thoughts. This patience can be nurtured in children if they understand the benefits it brings.

Our children can't grow alone. They rely on others for their wisdom, knowledge, and experience. They create new stories every day with new people they meet. Therefore, their growth is dependent on how well they can integrate with others in a way that makes them feel comfortable. They can only succeed if they learn to work with others and show patience towards those who are different from them.

How would you feel if your child was rejected by their peers or excluded from social gatherings for being different? Do you think their mental health would prosper? Do you think they would feel unloved or rejected? The only way to counter that rejection in a world dominated by racism and bias is by teaching them to have confidence in themselves while respecting each other's boundaries and embracing cultural and sociological differences. No good has ever come from one group of people putting another group down. Discrimination has done enough damage to the well-being of our children; it has taken away their choice to be themselves. Intolerance affects our goals, life choices, ambitions, and feelings of self-worth.

So how can we be sure that this doesn't happen to our children? We can do so by exposing them to different cultures, people, and environments where they can thrive with others together. We can offer them a world where they respect others and are respected by others. We can teach them how to take criticism and not feel offended or mad because someone else doesn't share the same ideas as them. We can teach them to respect each other's individuality and appreciate others for their uniqueness. Only then can we call ourselves proud parents, because we have taught our children two of the most essential of basic life skills, respect and empathy.

This ability to tolerate and respect each other's choices will help them throughout their whole life. When our children learn to value diversity they become better parents, have better morals and ideals, and form better relationships.

Respecting the boundaries and life choices of others also builds a child's self-esteem. When they learn to respect differences, they can embrace others more openly while maintaining a strong sense of self. They can let others be who they are without trying to change them. When they realize that others don't have to change for them, they also learn that they don't have to change for others either. This realization can make them more confident about their abilities and good qualities; this self-acceptance can result in them becoming more assertive, self-reliant, and confident. They can defend their beliefs without having to tear down the beliefs of others.

There are several ways you can help children internalize the concept of respecting personal boundaries. For starters, if they have questions about why other people look different from them, you must answer them honestly in a safe space. You must explain why others do things differently than them, eat different foods, practice different religions, or have different belief systems. The more open and communicative you are about diversity with your children, the less rude and nosey they will be.

Suppose your child comes up to you and asks why another child in the park is dressed differently than them. They have heard other kids leaving the less privileged kid out of their games, and they're not allowing him to take his turn on the swings.

How are you going to handle the situation? How are you going to make him understand that just because he is dressed differently doesn't mean he doesn't have the right to act like a child and enjoy his time in the park? You have to be extra careful about the words you choose and the explanations you provide, because this is going to be a valuable lesson if it's handled well.

Firstly, focus on positive things about that boy. His clothes might not be as nice as your child's, but does he seem friendly? Did he help you up when you fell down? Was he really good at playing hide-and-seek? If yes, then that's where you need to start from. Always highlight a new experience in a positive light so that your child understands that this isn't something they should run away from.

Second, reinforce good manners and kindness. When others are ignoring him, your child should make an effort to include him. If others are saying mean things, your child should say a nice thing.

Children aren't born with an awareness of social norms; they do what they observe others doing. Therefore, this is where you need to remind them to treat everyone with kindness and love regardless of how they are dressed. Encourage them to go up to the child and initiate a conversation. Encourage them to invite other kids to play with the boy too so that he doesn't feel excluded or different from them. This should teach your child about teamwork and empathy, which in turn teaches them to be respectful towards those who are different from them.

Finally, help them understand the reason why people are different from others. If the child happens to be from a different social class, take some time to learn about people from different socioeconomic backgrounds together. Once you do, explain to them how the boy was different and yet the same as them in many ways. You can read stories about their social or cultural group at bedtime, watch a movie featuring people from that group, or play games with characters that look like them. This will build acceptance and tolerance towards them. Present diversity in a new and positive light and as something that should be appreciated. Hopefully this will end their hesitation to talk to or include someone that doesn't look or act like them, and help your child to make others feel respected and valued.

Teaching Children to Respect Others

Teaching your child to respect everyone equally is necessary when setting healthy boundaries. This can be taught in many different ways and styles. The reason you must make learning and accepting diversity fun is so that repeated play can reinforce its importance and help internalize the lesson in children.

Become a Role Model

The first thing you must do is advocate for the beauty of differences. Children learn behaviors from you; if you show negativity towards a person or a group of people, your child is more likely to develop feelings of resentment towards them. Likewise, if you appreciate and welcome diversity in your life, they will too. So start by setting a good example for them to look up to. As stated before, you can bolster the message by helping them pick books, shows, and movies that celebrate diversity so that they stop being surprised or alarmed by different faces. Spread positive messages about how a difference of opinions doesn't mean there has to be conflict. You can show them that things can be handled respectfully even when there isn't an agreement to be reached. You can do so by sharing stories from your work or interacting with other people while out and about. Choose toys that represent and encompass people from different ethnicities to make them understand that we are all equal.

Exposure to New Experiences

Again, the goal here is to normalize diversity. Ideally, your child should not feel uncomfortable when seated with someone that looks different than them. It is easy to forget about the need for your child to experience newness when you meet the same people, drive around the same neighborhoods, or visit the same church or community center every day. Allow your child to step out of that bubble; instead of frequenting the exact same stores every week, take your child to a cultural food shop or a farmer's market with vendors from many different cultures. Similarly, you can encourage the celebration of different cultures and religions in your house by hosting gatherings and parties at your place. Find out what holidays your child's friends celebrate, and offer to help your child understand those holidays and the traditions they come from.

Teaching Skills and Values

Teach children skills like sign language, animal care, first-aid basics, and other skills so that they can be of assistance to everyone, not just the people they usually hang around with. Arrange playdates with children different from them so that they can become friends, develop empathy, and learn more about the world. Volunteer and donate to people who are less fortunate so that they can learn to be generous and kind to those who need some extra help. Spend time at a community center to help organize events, and spend time caring for animals at animal shelters. These are all great ways to teach kids to develop acceptance and embrace differences in addition to fostering important values and skills that will last a lifetime.

Chapter 5:

Explain the 'Whys'

Are all cows friends? Are there more chickens in the world than people? Are all babies brought by the stork? Why does Joshua look different than me? Why do Muslims pray five times a day? Why are there no flying cars?

Research into the inquisitive minds of children has revealed that the average child asks around seventy-three questions every day. Sounds exhausting, doesn't it? But that's how they learn about the world they live in. It's how they create, adapt to, and accept new experiences.

Another important aspect of healthy boundary-setting involves helping kids with their curiosity. The questions of why personal space matters, why other people have different opinions, and why we need to respect our elders (just to name a few) must all be handled wisely and answered meaningfully.

When children are growing, their perspectives about the world are expanding. They find something new to learn about every day, stumble upon new things and experiences frequently, and reenact the actions and behaviors they see others exhibiting. All these new experiences can raise many questions. When they ask you a question, they're seeking an answer they can understand and information they can add to their worldview. If you fail to provide them with an adequate answer, they are going to keep asking more questions until they can figure out a solution themselves and move on to the next thing.

Children ask specific questions because they want to piece information together. If your child asks why your phone sounds different when Dad calls versus when someone else calls, you might shrug it off and say it's not important. But you're forgetting, in this example, that to your child the answer may result in them forming associations between sounds, people, and technology. They are gradually making sense of the world as it is.

By nurturing their curiosity, we encourage confidence and good behavior. If they want to know why they shouldn't put a fork in an electric socket, an answer as simple as 'you'll get shocked' may not make much sense to them given that they have probably never been shocked before. You need to be more specific and explain to them how the socket connects to an electrical wire, what a shock feels like, and how creating a spark can cause a fire in the house. Make the danger real by saying that shocks hurt and that if they start a fire their toys could get burnt up.

Sometimes, hearing no repeatedly can cause a child to become even more curious. Be ready for this, be patient with your child, and answer them as best as you can.

It's your job to foster and nurture their curiosity while keeping them safe and helping them to expand their understanding of the world.

Why do Children Ask So Many Questions?

A child's environment has been shown to have a major impact on their growth. How many questions a child asks is often dependent upon the environment they were raised in. If the parents are always welcoming new experiences and encouraging independence in their children, the children tend to be more creative and better problem-solvers. They can handle different situations on their own by coming up with solutions from their mind. But that only partially answers this vital question. Why do they ask so many questions, and what can you do to nurture their creativity and self-confidence while encouraging critical thinking?

Children ask 'why' questions because it allows them to make sense of the world around them. Remember that your child is constantly experiencing brand new situations and stimuli. The questions and clarifications offered by parents spur and accelerate learning, and the right responses can prevent further questioning as the child feels capable of taking it on their own from there.

Sometimes kids ask endless questions because they are trying to seek attention. In his book *Questions Are the Answer: A Breakthrough Approach to Your Most Vexing Problems at Work and in Life,* Hal Gregerson writes that a child might not ask questions because they didn't understand your answers the first time or because they weren't listening carefully. A child will often ask questions repeatedly because they want your attention and time. They want to be close to you and to feel important and loved. They ask questions because the action keeps you engaged and interested in what they are doing. This prevents them from feeling anxiety, which can happen when a child feels like their parents aren't present mentally and emotionally.

Finally, a healthy curiosity about knowing everything about everything shapes a child's basic understanding of the world. It builds their vocabulary and teaches them how to effectively communicate and comprehend things unfamiliar to them. The following section discusses the many ways in which you can help to foster this curiosity.

How to Handle a Child's Curiosity

The activities discussed below are useful to help cultivate that sense of curiosity within boundaries in children from an early age. The more knowledgeable they are about the social behaviors expected of them, the better they will fare. They will grow up to be responsible adults who respect one another and their need for personal space.

Weekly Reminders

Be prepared to answer the same questions over and over again, as children need reinforcement to cement new concepts in their minds (and sometimes they just plain forget the answer to a question asked already). If you want them to follow personal boundary rules, it is best to make a game out of it. Once a week, sit down with your child and review the rules and expectations for anything from house rules to respecting others; treat it like a game show, with little prizes for correct answers. Be prepared to offer further clarification if they miss out on important points. Help them combat confusion and anxiety by preparing them on how to handle different social scenarios before they occur. Sometimes children misunderstand what is being told to them. Repetition helps to clear the message in their minds and prepares them to tackle things independently.

Explain Things

Make it a habit to offer as much explanation as your child needs. According to another study, the reason children repeat questions and ask them so often is that they want further details and insight into the thing they're curious about (Frazier et al., 2009). It isn't just to annoy you or cause you stress. A thorough answer may prevent further questioning, but it may also require repetition and clarification later (which isn't necessarily a bad thing). Once they are satisfied with the information provided, there will hopefully be fewer repetitions of the exact same question.

Accept and Research

If they seem troubled by a thought or question and no explanations provided by you seem to make sense to them, encourage them to research the topic on their own. If they are old enough to use a search engine, ask them to research their query and seek answers. If you don't have the answer to a particular question they asked, don't dismiss it altogether. Instead, accept that you don't know the answer and research it together. When your child sees that you are motivated to seek an answer for something you don't know, it will encourage them to do the same. Soon they will be researching answers to their creative questions themselves. At the same time, encourage them to read books or watch documentaries that provide answers. This will cultivate the habit of reading and exploration, which is an enriching and valuable lifelong habit.

What Do You Think?

Finally, instead of providing answers straight away, ask them what they think the answer could be. Why do they think they should maintain some distance from others? Why do they think some people wear different clothes? Why do they think that we shouldn't hit or push others? Turning the question back onto them encourages creative thinking. It allows them to problem-solve and encourages them to come up with imaginative explanations while nurturing further curiosity.

Chapter 6:

Role-Play

Have you ever noticed your toddler picking up the phone and pretending to make a call? Have you noticed them mimic the way you sip your tea or the voice you make when you're talking to a pet? Have you ever wondered what they are trying to do?

The answer is that they are engaging in the valuable practice of role-play.

Role-play involves small scenarios, often hypothetical, where you imagine yourself in a situation, design the pretend world around you, and determine what your next plan of action will be. When you use role-play to help set healthy boundaries for children, you might ask them to imagine a scenario where someone has crossed a boundary. This step is like putting everything you have learned so far to the test, but in a safe space where the play can stop at any time. With effective role-playing games and activities, you can determine how much your child knows, how they handle emotions, and how they think. Role-playing allows them to take up the role of someone different, usually the central character in a situation, and encourages them to decide what they would do next in the scenario.

Role-play can be designed to practice boundary-setting abilities. You can use role-playing games to teach children how to appear engaged, make proper eye contact, and deal with social situations with confidence. Using a small bit of free time each day or each week to encourage the expression of emotions and ideas is an enriching and important activity.

Role-playing comes in three types, including occupational, real-life situations, and fantasy-based play. In occupational role-play, young children pretend to be someone with an occupation such as doctor, firefighter, police officer, or scientist. They imagine themselves in an occupational setting of their choosing and pretend to perform their duties. It is both fun and inspirational, as children get to be who they are most inspired by. They also learn that it is important to help everyone regardless of who they are. By engaging in a fantasy occupation, children can naturally develop effective communication skills as well as problem-solving.

In real-life situation role-playing, children get to take on real-life situations in a safe and comfortable environment. This kind of play helps children to explore and investigate situations they may have observed happening around them or to others. Examples of real-life role-playing scenarios can range from positive experiences such as pretending to go shopping to the negative and scary, such as pretending to go through an earthquake.

In fantasy-based role-play scenarios, children get to be someone they see in movies or read about in stories.

There's no limit to the scenarios a child might come up with, from pretending to be animals to pretending to be superheroes. Usually children create scenarios in which they can become or emulate their role models and heroes, fantastical or otherwise. This type of play encourages extensive use of the imagination as well as storytelling and teamwork. Through fantasy-based role-play with others, children must work together in order to drive their invented story forward, which can in turn teach them about confidence, creativity, and respect for others.

Importance of Role-Play in A Child's Life

Imaginative scenarios foster creativity. It is known to promote better performance in school, since the child feels equipped and confident to handle any situation they are presented with. They can stand up for one another and reduce the likelihood of being bullied or taken advantage of. As they grow older, such skills can help them deal with different types of people in the professional world and learn to live with them peacefully.

In addition, role-play also encourages the development of cognitive skills and abilities. Children learn how to think for themselves and decrease their dependence on others. In a world which can seem to be dominated by corruption and ill intent, it is important that your child feels prepared and safe. Pretend play also allows for free expression. Children can live in their imaginative world where anything is possible.

Imaginative play also fosters emotional and social development. Children can develop empathy and learn to sympathize with others. They learn about emotional self-regulation as well as how to take criticism and provide feedback without hurting anyone's feelings. They also learn to cope with negative emotions in healthy ways, alleviating anxiety and stress.

Role-playing empowers children to become independent. This is beneficial for both the parent and the child; by enacting and taking up roles of different characters, they can make spur-of-the-moment decisions without the need for assistance or guidance from an adult. Becoming self-reliant is a great skill to develop in children today as it prepares them for the world tomorrow.

Role-playing also helps to build the vocabulary. By playing in different scenarios, children are essentially writing their own stories and using what they've learned and absorbed to flesh out both the world and the character they're inhabiting. Playing together with others allowed for teaching and learning between children, as well as a sharing of ideas and creative thinking. In the process, they're even able to learn valuable new skills and information. For example, in role-playing a doctor's office scenario, a child might treat an imaginary broken bone or scraped knee and develop an interest in the field of medicine. If one child has a parent who works as a firefighter, that child will likely be able to teach other children about all the things a firefighter does through play. A child who lines up all their dolls and stuffed animals and 'teaches' them mathematics might be sowing the seeds for a career in education.

All these skills and life lessons are easily learned when paired with play. These activities can also promote healthy social interactions with people their age, which can go hand-in-hand with a child's developing sense of social norms and respect for boundaries.

Role-Play Activities to Promote Healthy Boundaries

What If...

'What if' scenarios are a great way to teach children how they can handle situations independently without any assistance from adults. It can also teach them how to react and respond wisely and respectfully to others. Hypothetical scenarios can help shape their behavior and perspectives. They will provide insights to you about their personality and emotions. Below are some 'what if' scenarios you can discuss and act out with your children in their free time to see what their reaction would be.

- What if you saw your best friend being bullied?
- What if someone wrongly accused you of stealing at school?
- What if your teacher disregarded your opinion and went with an idea presented by someone else?
- What if you were not invited to a party all your friends were going to?
- What if someone tried to kiss or hug you without your permission?
- What if a stranger tried to talk to you and asked you to get in their car?

All these questions and many others similar to them can serve as great discussion topics in which you can learn about how emotionally intelligent and respectful your child is. If most of their answers suggest angry outbursts, arguments, or disrespect towards others, it can be a great opportunity to change the way they see things and develop empathy.

How Would You React if...

This is quite similar to the exercise discussed above. The only difference is that in this exercise the focus is more on a child's physical response or reaction to a certain situation. The goal is to understand their thought processes and how prepared they are to deal with unexpected situations. You begin by giving them scenarios where they have to decide between two different actions and explain why. For example, if someone in their class keeps calling them ugly or stupid, what would they do? Would they stand up for themselves or let the bullying continue?

How would you react if…

- Someone tried to snatch your lunch from your hands?
- Someone stood too close to you when they spoke?
- Someone pushed you on purpose?
- Someone tried to disregard your feelings?
- You were made fun of on the school bus by a bunch of mean kids?

Answering these questions will give you insights into how they view the violation of personal boundaries and how they would react in situations like these.

how they feel when their physical or emotional limits are tested. As such, we need to be more vigilant than ever, especially as cases of harassment and child sexual abuse are on the rise. By ignoring this incredibly important issue we are unintentionally raising a generation that thinks that their bodies aren't theirs to control. They grow up thinking that it is okay to be treated in unwanted ways and that they must remain silent. Such feelings can easily lead to depression and a lack of self-esteem and self-love.

This is one of the many reasons why it is important to talk about personal space as well as physical and emotional boundaries early on. We must teach our children that it isn't disrespectful to say no when it benefits our mental and emotional health, and it all starts at home. After all, if we can't make them feel comfortable in their own house and surroundings, how can we expect them to feel in control of their own bodies out in the world?

In this final chapter we will discuss an important topic regarding physical and emotional boundaries and their importance in a child's life. Planting the idea that our bodies belong only to us in the early years of their development allows them to have a final say in who they feel comfortable with. Teaching them about healthy physical and emotional boundaries creates an opportunity for them to understand what healthy boundaries look like and how they can enforce them without sounding rude or disrespectful.

A physical boundary is an invisible boundary that comprises a set of personal rules that determine a good and bad touch. This knowledge about what type of physical touch is acceptable and what isn't allows kids to take control of their bodies and learn to say no when they sense someone is trying to violate those boundaries.

Physical boundaries are essential because they help children to define the self. They can choose to decide what they are comfortable with, and they become aware of their own rights. Boundaries and rules about the body teach kids how they deserve to be treated by others. With these rules they can draw a clearer picture of their limits, needs, and desires. If they feel violated, they can reach out to someone for help. However, if they are unaware of those limits, they might begin to consider those behaviors and actions by others as normal behavior and allow the abuse to continue. Therefore, setting clear physical boundaries early can prevent cases of sexual violence and domestic abuse that children might never dare to speak about. With clear boundaries and safe spaces in place, children can become aware of the things they and others are responsible for, and how what happens with them doesn't have to become a bad memory.

Physical boundaries relate to our need for personal space, comfortable touch, and essential needs like food, rest, water, and exercise. Established boundaries allow children to draw a line and assertively prevent someone from touching them inappropriately or trying to push their body's limits. For instance, if a child feels tired and wants to rest, they should be able to do so because that is what their body is telling them they need. In this instance, forcing the child to continue working prevents them from listening to their body and can lead to them overworking themselves.

Some examples of communicating healthy physical boundaries include the following:

- I need to sleep. I am extremely tired.
- I have a headache and need to lie down.
- I don't feel like eating because this vegetable makes me feel nauseous.
- I don't like to be hugged because it invades my personal space and I am not comfortable with it.
- No, I don't want to be kissed on the cheek.
- Please don't enter my room without asking for my permission first.

Being denied the right to set healthy physical boundaries can lead to emotional and mental distress. It makes children think that they have no say in how they want to be treated, which can make them feel helpless and vulnerable.

Emotional boundaries include a person's mental and emotional health. They include limitations on how much we want to share with someone and how much we wish not to disclose. For example, many of us will avoid talking about a new relationship with our colleagues or friends because it wasn't the time or place to bring it up. Violations of emotional boundaries happen when someone chooses to belittle, criticize, or demean us. It happens when someone chooses to invalidate how we feel.

Emotional boundaries for children are all about respecting and honoring how they feel or what they are going through. It involves showing concern, but not taking control from them. When you teach your children to set healthy emotional boundaries, you are essentially teaching them to recognize and label their emotions and become aware of how much they can healthily take in. Emotional boundaries give them the choice to hold back or share information, and limit sharing too much with those they don't know well or who won't respond well. Respecting your child's emotional boundaries means that you validate their feelings and emotions and respect their ability to take in emotional information.

Some examples of communicating strong emotional boundaries include:

- I don't share my feelings with you because you criticize me as a response and it makes me feel shut out. I can only share what I feel with you if you promise to respect my feelings.
- I wish I could help you in some way, but currently I don't feel like I am in the right state to help you or take in this information. If you would excuse me, I would appreciate it if you would discuss this matter with someone else.

- I am having a difficult time with my emotions and would like to vent it out. Do you have the time and patience to hear me out or would another time or person be better?

Why Children Are Afraid to Set Healthy Physical and Emotional Boundaries

One reason children are so afraid to set healthy physical and emotional boundaries is that from the minute they were born the world has told them that they have to be people pleasers. We pass them around from relative to relative to hold and kiss, we dress them up in outfits they haven't picked based on what we think is cute or charming, and we trot them out to events they find boring for friends and strangers to coo at them. Rarely have we given them the permission to be themselves. The unfortunate reality is that all these actions tell them it doesn't matter if you don't like to be hugged; you have to allow it because it's your grandfather and it would be rude to decline. We have implied that the welfare and happiness of others is more important than our children's, and that if they choose to disobey it comes off as offensive and rude. In the process, our children end up getting hurt without our knowledge or intention.

Setting Healthy Physical and Emotional Boundaries

This rather sad realization suggests that we are raising individuals who have no idea about their needs and limitations, let alone how to fulfill them. Violation of personal space can be uncomfortable and lead to fallout and anxiety in relationships. If your child can't trust you to share their discomfort, who else can they turn to?

Below are some ideas to promote discussion with your child in creative ways. Take a look yourself and see if you and your child are ready to have a conversation about physical and emotional boundaries.

Let Them Decide For Themselves

Allow them the freedom to be who they are and to decide how they want to carry themselves. From picking their clothes to being around people they feel most comfortable and safe with, let them choose how they want to live their lives. All you have to do is support them in their decision to take the lead. For example, if they tell you that they don't want to shake hands with someone, listen to them. Ask them why they feel that way about that person in particular. Instead of merely insisting that they should shake hands, teach them the following gestures and sentences to use in place of physical contact:

- Wave from a distance

- Smile and nod
- "I don't like to shake hands, but I am glad we met."

These don't come off as rude or offensive. Furthermore, be sure to tell them to not feel guilty about their actions, and that they don't need to apologize for putting their physical needs first. Their happiness and comfort are extremely important, and they have every right to set physical boundaries for themselves.

Encourage the use of the word 'no' even when they say it to you. Don't act offended or try to discipline them. Instead, sit down with them and inquire why they declined your request. The reason they don't want to take a bath right now could be because they are tired or not in the mood. Discuss when would be a better time for it and compromise from there.

Role-Playing Emotionally Triggering Scenarios

Again, role-playing can aid in helping young ones deal with their emotions healthily. Using this technique, you can teach them how to respond and react better to emotionally triggering situations where they feel belittled, demeaned, or out of control due to anger. Create a What If scenario where your child gets into an argument with someone who called them an unkind name. Ask them how it would make them feel. They'll likely say they would feel hurt or angry. What will they do next? Would they wait out and let their emotional state return to a peaceful one or engage in a fight or worse, call the other person an unkind word too? If you have taught them about healthy boundaries, they are more likely to choose the first option.

To prevent this from happening in the first place, teach your child alternative ways to handle tough situations. Establish a script of peaceful dialogue so that a boundary can be established for the next time. Ask them to go up to the pretend person and ask them to speak about the argument, in the presence of a trusted adult if necessary. Ensure your child knows to own up to any wrongdoing if necessary. Then, tell the imagined person that name-calling is not acceptable and that they would prefer to have a more respectful conversation the next time around.

Conclusion

Without boundaries, children may grow up to be manipulative to their parents and others to get everything they want. Worse, they may not understand that their body is theirs to give others permission to touch or be near as they like. This is why setting boundaries in a child's life is vital for their development as empathetic and compassionate human beings. It helps them understand the importance of self-restraint and how to express themselves in a manner where they won't harm anyone else while doing so.

Personal space is important for our personal and emotional health. When we are in the presence of people we are close to, it allows us to be comfortable and express ourselves to the best of our ability. Children with a healthy sense of personal space tend to have more confidence, higher self-esteem, and are more open and friendly with one another. They are more likely to get along well with others. Having healthy personal space can even help a person manage their emotional reaction when experiencing strong feelings such as anger or sadness.

Therefore, parents should use this guide as a basis to begin training their children about healthy boundary setting. They should encourage kindness and empathy towards others, and teach children to respect each other's opinions and life choices. Healthy boundaries can help children master social skills like effective communication, body language detection, and active listening. It can help them learn how to be assertive and state their needs with confidence. It teaches them how to take control of their mental, emotional, and physical health by maintaining control over their body. It teaches them why it's okay to say 'no' and to not allow others to walk all over them.

Thank you for giving this book a read. I hope you loved reading it as much as I enjoyed writing it. It would make me the happiest person on earth if you would take a moment to leave an honest review. All you have to do is visit the site where you purchased this book: It's that simple! The review doesn't have to be a full-fledged paragraph; a few words will do. Your few words will help others decide if this is what they should be reading as well. Thank you in advance, and best of luck with your parenting adventures. Every moment is a joyous one with a child.

References

5 ways to teach kids how to respect personal space. (n.d.). www.brainbalancecenters.com. https://www.brainbalancecenters.com/blog/ways-to-teach-kids-how-to-understand-privacy-and-personal-space

Campbell, L. (2021, June 8). *Personal boundaries: Types and how to set them.* Psych Central. https://psychcentral.com/lib/what-are-personal-boundaries-how-do-i-get-some#takeaway

Castro, D. T. (2015, August 18). *Setting rules and limits for young children.* CCE Suffolk County Family Health & Wellness. https://blogs.cornell.edu/ccesuffolkfhw/2015/08/18/setting-rules-and-limits-for-young-children/

Connor, E. (2018, May 23). *This is the real reason kids ask "why" so much -- and what to do about it.* Scary Mommy. https://www.scarymommy.com/why-do-children-ask-why/

Earnshaw, E. (2019, July 20). *6 types of boundaries you deserve to have (and how to maintain them).* Mindbodygreen. https://www.mindbodygreen.com/articles/six-types-of-boundaries-and-what-healthy-boundaries-look-like-for-each

Five reasons why role play is important for early years! (2020, February 17). Newbyleisure.com. https://newbyleisure.com/blog/2020-02-17-five-reasons-why-role-play-is-important-for-early-years

Frazier, B. N., Gelman, S. A., & Wellman, H. M. (2009). Preschoolers' search for explanatory information within adult-child conversation. *Child Development*, *80*(6), 1592–1611. https://doi.org/10.1111/j.1467-8624.2009.01356.x

Guidelines for setting rules. (n.d.). Advocare Main Line Pediatrics. http://www.advocaremainlinepeds.com/Resources/Healthy-Kids,-Happy-Kids/Discipline/Guidelines-for-Setting-Rules

Hardy, R. (2018). *Why do kids ask so many questions?* Curiousworld.com. https://www.curiousworld.com/blog/why-do-kids-ask-so-many-questions

How to teach your children to respect differences. (2018, September 17). You Are Mom. https://youaremom.com/parenting/children-respect-differences/

Innis, G. (2012, December 31). *Personal space: A social skill children need and adults can teach.* MSU Extension. https://www.canr.msu.edu/news/personal_space_a_social_skill_children_need_and_adults_can_teach

King, P. (2020). *Establishing boundaries : How to protect yourself, become assertive, take back control, and set yourself free.* Independently Published.

Lau, C. (2016, June 16). *5 ways to teach our children body boundaries - fractus learning.* Https://Www.fractuslearning.com/. https://www.fractuslearning.com/teach-children-body-boundaries/

Lee, K. (2021, April 1). *Strategies for setting healthy boundaries for kids.* Verywell Family. https://www.verywellfamily.com/whos-the-boss-how-to-set-healthy-boundaries-for-kids-3956403

Levin, N. (2021). *Setting boundaries will set yoiu free: The ultimate guide to telling the truth, creating connection.. , and finding freedom.* Hay House Uk Ltd.

Minocha, A. (2016, February 29). *How to teach children about personal space.* Flintobox. https://flintobox.com/blog/parenting/how-to-teach-children-about-personal-space

Palacios, R. (2016, February 19). *Why do children ask, "why?"* HuffPost. https://www.huffpost.com/entry/why-do-children-ask-why_b_9233266

Pulido-Tobiassen, D., & Gonzalez-Mena, J. (1999). Teaching diversity: A place to begin. *Early Childhood Today.*

Reasons why role playing is important for your child. (n.d.). PBC Expo Shop. https://www.pbcexpo.com.au/blog/reasons-why-role-playing-is-important-for-your-child

Robson, D. (n.d.). *How to teach kids about personal space.* And next Comes L - Hyperlexia Resources. Retrieved August 9, 2021, from https://www.andnextcomesl.com/2017/03/how-to-teach-kids-about-personal-space.html

Sandstrom, H., & Huerta, S. (2013). The negative effects of instability on child development: A research synthesis. In Urban Institute. The Urban Institute. https://www.urban.org/sites/default/files/pub

lication/32706/412899-The-Negative-Effects-of-Instability-on-Child-Development-A-Research-Synthesis.PDF

Slutsky, A. (2011). *Fun ways to teach students classroom rules | synonym.* Synonym.com. https://classroom.synonym.com/fun-teach-students-classroom-rules-8745796.html

Teach your child to respect differences. (2010, September 30). Moms Who Think. https://www.momswhothink.com/teach-your-child-to-respect-differences/

Teaching children about respecting differences – thrive. (2020, August 7). Thrive.psu.edu. https://thrive.psu.edu/blog/teaching-children-about-respecting-differences/

Teaching kids about personal space and boundaries. (2020, January 13). Amelio Blog. https://www.amelio.in/amelio-blog/2020/01/13/teaching-kids-about-personal-space-and-boundaries/

Whitener, S. (2019, December 11). *Council post: How setting boundaries positively impacts your self-esteem.* Forbes. https://www.forbes.com/sites/forbescoachesc ouncil/2019/12/11/how-setting-boundaries-positively-impacts-your-self-esteem/?sh=68ef45a0339c

Wiatrak, B. (2019, May 10). *Teaching young children to respect & accept diversity.* The Cultured Baby. https://theculturedbaby.world/2019/05/09/te ach-young-children-to-respect-and-accept-diversity/

Wilkes, F. (2018, March 6). *5 reasons why role play is important for kids.* Conscious Craft. https://consciouscraft.uk/blogs/news/5-reason-why-role-playing-is-important-for-kids

www.ingramcontent.com/pod-product-compliance
Lightning Source LLC
LaVergne TN
LVHW051428080426
835508LV00022B/3286